CRYSTALS
TO
MANIFEST

For Dani, the brightest of lights,
the greatest of hearts.

EMMA LUCY KNOWLES

CRYSTALS TO MANIFEST

HARNESS THE POWER OF CRYSTALS & START LIVING YOUR BEST LIFE

EBURY
PRESS

CONTENTS

INTRODUCTION

It's easy to think of manifesting as a new phenomenon, but many religious or faith-based practices have worked with manifestation or the law of attraction for centuries, so, just like crystals, manifestation is not a passing fad. With this book in your hand I want to empower you to honour and hone your manifesting abilities – using crystals in your practice – to harness their awesome power, and yours.

There can be a tendency to look at manifestation as the answer to all our problems, using it to focus on material gain. 'If I just "want" that new job/car/relationship hard enough it will fall into my lap.' If we approach manifestation like this, it's very easy to become frustrated and you'll likely quit when it 'lets you down' and doesn't immediately deliver what you've asked for.

It's important to remember that, as with all practices, we need to take the time to lay the groundwork, to tune into our mind, body and being in order to set our intentions. We need to fully commit to attracting into our life that which we choose to will into existence, and to resonate with what we desire and deserve – and then manifest or attract that back to us. The aim of this book is to show you exactly how to do that: how to align your energy – not just your thoughts and wishes – to **clear the way** of what might have been holding you back, to **cast out** new intentions to the universe, and **call back** those things you want to change and those you wish to see created.

So, I welcome you to your manifestation manifesto; your guide to using crystals to harness your best life and heighten your greatest sense of self.

PART 1

WHAT IS MANIFESTING?

Clear Quartz

It's near impossible to define this in one sentence but in essence, manifestation is the process of bringing something tangible into your life through the universal law of attraction. With the practice of manifesting we are creating our lives. Just as we are what we eat and what we think, we can also become that which we feel. So to harness that power, we have to become an active participant in our manifestation practice and we do this by feeling something on every level – through our actions, words and thoughts – and then the belief in its creation.

Manifesting as we know it today really broke ground in the New Thought movement in the nineteenth century. These days we can be so quick to label things as 'trends', and in doing so we write them off as things that aren't serious, meaning we inadvertently oversimplify and squash the essence of beautiful ancient practices. Manifestation is not simply asking the universe for what we want. It is an enactment of personal power, a direction of energy, a structured (yet fun) practice, a way of being and living, a way of energetically communicating and acting, of growing, learning, healing and calling into your life all that you deserve or that which is for your upmost good. You manifest to achieve that which will fulfill you and keep you vibrating energetically in a way that feels awesome inside and out. This then creates more of that good feeling and in turn brings you tangible results; the emotional feel-good and yes, even the material gain. Throughout the book I will describe this as 'for your highest good'. Your highest good is the link between you, Mother Earth and your spirit – that part of you that 'just knows'. Through these pages we will be developing that part of yourself so you can be effortlessly discerning about what feels good – truly good for you – with total ease.

Rose Quartz, Clear Quartz

Labradorite

WHAT'S MY ENERGY GOT TO DO WITH IT?

The universe and everything in it is made of energy – a powerful force, that reaches beyond where our minds can travel. It's made up of a multitude of spectrums, frequencies and textures. Every living being within it has its own micro-universe, vibrating at different frequencies that add to and affect this miraculous tapestry of energy. The rate and the speed of your vibration can govern your mood, your thoughts and your decision-making. When we are happy and buzzing, we emit high vibes or higher frequency levels, and when we are burnt out and down we emit lower vibes. When our vibration is 'low', our energy feels less impactful and in that state we tend not to feel so great in our skin. When our energy is wild, we tend to feel uneven: in a state of constantly chasing the next buzz and never being able to really harness it. You need a balance in your energy: for example, a balanced dose of the fire in your energy can move and drive you just as a balanced dose of water in your energy can allow you to be sensitive to yourself and the needs of others. Working closely with your energy and tending to it, means that over time you can start to influence, affect or control it more impactfully.

Amazonite, Pyrite, Lepidolite & Hematite

To allow us to comprehend your true vibrational power, imagine your body as an empty test tube. Take out all the stuff you think and know about yourself and see yourself as a clear and empty vessel. Now fill that space with powerful particles or energy. Envision them as bubbles the size of marbles. Next imagine a little fizz, a little movement between the particles – this is your life force. Just as heat or fire creates boiling water, this life force starts to move from your belly and radiates all the way out through you and beyond you. It begins choreographing all those particles so that they create a knock-on effect of momentum and bounce and vibe, at multiple speeds and in multiple directions, which becomes a creative force. That creative force is an an energy language that is unique to you and it has the power to move from you and through your aura into the energy and particles of the universe. Your energy is like a unique wifi signal, the vibration is the message in the signal and calls out to those people who are signalling on the same wave length as you. Just like a wave, your signal is in constant motion. So where do these waves go? What's the direction of travel? In essence, like attracts like and if the frequency of your energy is where you feel good, your energy will head out in that direction seeking that which is seeking you. If you feel good and right in yourself, the wave will pull you towards the right people and the right conversations. You'll 'attract them', you will eat the right foods, listen to songs and conversations, digest TV and media that feel good, you will be manifesting goodness into your life – every minute.

WHAT ARE CRYSTALS AND HOW DO THEY SUPPORT MANIFESTATION?

Crystals are more like us than we may think. They are undeniably beautiful, they come in all shapes and sizes, some of them we will like, others we will love and some will just not be on our radar as we don't vibe with them... until one day we do. Crystals can be some of the best friends you will ever have in your life but, like the stranger you pass in the street, there is more to them than meets the eye and their part in our manifestation of life and being is key.

Amethyst Geode

Crystals are so powerful because they work towards connecting and aligning us to a power and energy that at times is unseen. At the same time, they encourage us to connect to, and heighten, our own personal power by reflecting that internal sparkle of self, even if it feels lost or hidden to us at times.

So how do they rock? Well crystals are formed under years of pressure and they can do more than one thing at any one time. Like us, they are energy, they vibrate, they can give and they can take. Crystals act as both lenses and filters, they can cleanse, charge and empower you.

Just as with manifesting, these crystal beauties are not the new kids on the block – they too have been used by a multitude of faiths and religious practices throughout time as offerings of loving commitment. Each crystal's energy vibrates at its own rate and, just like us, its vibe is shaped by where and how it was formed, with no two (even the same type of crystal) ever the same. This means that they also each give off a highly unique signal which is sometimes punchy and sometimes a more subtle vibrational pulse. These different vibrations resonate with certain feelings, emotions and energies that we feel or would like to feel. So just as you have a friend who lifts you up when you feel down, a friend you call for a laugh, a friend to give you confidence – you can have a crystal friend to go to in your time of need. The superpower of their vibration is that it has the ability to influence and affect the flow of energy in to and out of our being. They connect us on a deeper or higher level with that which we are ready to call in to our lives, or simply put, manifest!

As I've said, crystals act as lenses and filters for our life's energy – they can be used not only to draw out that which no longer serves us, that which we no longer need – they can also work to draw forth that which we desire, that we wish to be more abundant in, be it emotional or physical.

It's super important to build a relationship and practise with your crystals in a way that feels good to you – you are of course the one in the driving seat of your own life. Please always remember that working with crystals, connecting to your energy and manifesting your life is a unique practice and how you work with them, use them and how they feel to you will be very different to how they feel to your friend. In getting to know them we can develop an even more enriching relationship with ourselves.

How crystals work with our being is beautiful. Universal energy, life force or qi (however you name it) flows through our body and being via our energy centres or chakras. We have seven main centres/chakras that run along the length of the body and each governs a particular internal solar system, from our connection to life, to our emotions and personal power, through to the way we love or allow ourselves to be loved, the way we communicate (the words we speak to

Black Obsidian

ourselves and to others), to how we visualise and create life within and around us, and how we connect with the universe and each other. The chakras are these sensational vortexs of energy and light that spin widely, pulsing to effectively push and pull energy to and from our being. They filter that which no longer serves us energetically and pull in that which sets our heart and soul on fire.

When these energy centres are in balance, each centre is spinning as wide open as the next, in perfect harmony, in a clockwise direction. When someone hurts us, emotionally, or physically, the energy centre that corresponds to the formation or direction of that energetic pain starts to protect itself and, just like a turtle shrinking back into its shell, your energy starts to spin in an anti-clockwise direction. Some people may say you are 'blocked' at these times – but for me that word feels far too dramatic and it can heighten the worry that you are not going to be able to move forward from this space or feeling. Look at it this way, when you are in love your heart energy is spinning wide and free, balanced, then another heart energy joins in your spiral, connects with your flow and together you open each other's hearts further and wider. When that love concludes, grows old, or someone breaks that trust – the energy between the two beings is disconnected (though not totally). As a result, our heart centre feels less full or 'broken' because the energy that once added to our essence has now all but 'gone' – if you haven't made that decision yourself and made peace with it, it feels like a plug has been abruptly pulled from its socket. So how do we heal, balance and manifest love again in these times? It's about trusting in the vibration of love, believing you can manifest that for yourself again, that you create it. This is when your crystal saviours step in.

Crystals work on both ends of the spectrum, they draw in what we need or are ready for and they pull out from our depths all that is no longer serving us. At this time, crystals step into their power as energy lenses and, just like a pair of prescription glasses, they adjust the energy for the wearer's benefit. The crystal lenses act as an energy filter – as the universal energy pours down upon one of your energy centres, it hits the lens and starts to shift into alignment with that centre's frequency.

When your body is aligned, in harmony – supported energetically – you become a magnet for miracles. You become a receptive tower of force as much as a super signal, creating every moment of your life from a vibrational frequency of your making. You can then use that force, that energy, not just to offer clarity – but to draw in, to manifest and attract clearly that which is for your highest good.

Carnelian

HOW DO WE TRUST IN THE MANIFESTATION PROCESS?

We live in an increasingly immediate world. Forgotten to buy milk? Can't muster the energy to walk to the shop or make dinner? You can have your milk and your meal delivered to your door in minutes. Want to buy a new book? You can download and start reading it in seconds. Don't like your outfit for tomorrow night? One click and it's on the doormat. Because of this, we can feel frustrated when we are made to wait for the things we want, especially if we're not even sure they're on their way to us in the first place. So, how do we trust that the manifestation process is working for us?

I have three magical ingredients for the manifestation mix: patience, passion and faith. As long as you have, and work on, these three things, you will feel more grounded, more centred and be more able to trust in your manifestation practice and most importantly, yourself. Trust in the feeling of knowing it is on its way.

Here are some quick-flash personal highlights that I try to remind myself of when I am feeling frustrated in my practice (which, before you start kicking yourself, is very normal):

— One day I decided I was going to write a book – pretty much out of nowhere I just felt it. I didn't know how or why and then one year later my heavenly publisher reached out with my first book offer. I turned it down (old fashioned imposter syndrome) six months later it came back round to me and I said yes – it was for my highest good and I know that now!

— My patience was rewarded when, as a ten-year-old I told my mum I was going to make jewellery out of crystals, and she dismissed it as a childish ambition. Cut to twenty-five years later I have my own jewellery and crystal line.

— My adolescent passion (ok *obsession!*) with The Beatles came full circle when I graduated and, at a loss for what to do, landed a job with The Beatles' management company (best first job ever).

Before we go any further, it's important to note that this is my highlights reel. In between these mega moments have been some real losses and low points: grief, loss, redundancy, fear, abuse, feelings of entrapment and loss of self. Just as we all do, I had to work to find my light, found disappointment when what I wanted didn't land, and raged at the universe when I felt it didn't show up for me. But as we journey through to find what's right and what's good for ourselves, we heal and we lean into the good energy we find in life. It's so important to track the highlights as the mind will always be sure to remember those lower moments.

Kyanite, Carnelian

PART 2

Rainbow Fluorite

IT
BEGINS
WITH
YOU

So, is manifesting as simple as ask, believe, receive? And if that's the case, I can have whatever I want because the universe always delivers, right? Well, yes, that's the theory – there is however more that needs to go into the practice. I need to stress just how important it is that you are clear and ready, not just to receive what you desire, but to ask for it.

The vibrations of our bodies, minds, emotions, egos, spirits and souls are powerful forces, and these parts of ourself create our reality so we need to make sure these energies are aligned with our manifestation practice. In other words, you need to be energetically ready to send out for, and then receive, that which you are asking for.

This is where your crystals come back in. Crystals, as we know, have the ability to realign our energies and vibrations back to their purest quality and tone, and set the frequency of our 'highest good'. We want to start working with them to give ourselves a daily, weekly or monthly vibrational MOT – regularly refueling and purifying our energy to give ourselves a better chance to avoid a crash and burnout.

This is the empowering part of manifestation. This is where we get to **clear the way** energetically, **cast out** for that which we are willing to receive and **call in** or manifest it into reality. I'm going to come back to these expressions a lot so let's have a look at what I mean by them. As with many spiritual practices, it all starts with an intention.

YOUR LENS OF INTENTION

Intention is the way we act to purposefully effect a desired result and it plays a key role in the manifestation process. If our intention is unclear in any scenario, if the thoughts are murky, or the belief isn't there – our lens becomes clouded and the magnetic attraction weakened. Now, when the mind is clearer, our daily thoughts resonate with who we truly are – and in turn our intention becomes crystallised and sharp, and the way ahead feels clearer (even if you can't quite see it yet).

By way of example from my personal life, is a belief that I am not seen, specifically not seen for who I truly am. As a lightworker, a spirit whisperer and the like – I was never taught clearly who I was – it wasn't what we would call 'normal' to be me, there weren't other 'mes' around that I could see myself in, other than people who were mocked for being 'woo woo'... As such, on one hand I couldn't really see myself in the world and on the other I didn't want to be seen because I didn't want to be laughed at, so in turn the habitual vibration became 'I can't see myself' or 'Please don't see me'. These merged and evolved into a super strong intention, a powerful belief, and so a signal was cast out with that message and my belief attracted that invisibility right back.

CLEAR THE WAY

Clearing the way is what we will do with our almighty crystal squad. It's not just about the way ahead – life and energy aren't quite so linear – it's every direction: the future, the past and the present. 'The way' is the future but most importantly it's the right here and now. It's the way in, the way through and the way out. Just like in a city, 'the way' is not a straight road, but rather an intricate network with junctions, roundabouts and turnings. We can choose to change direction, change lanes, take it at our own pace – as long as the road is clear we can feel empowered to explore. But if there's traffic, if there are things getting in the way, it becomes harder to explore our life's true purpose. As with the example of my clouded lens, several beliefs merged to create one strong mega and blocking intention, which I had to work to dissolve in order to clear the way to being seen.

CAST OUT

Our words are like magical spells – each word fires out an energy in association with it. Remember those little marbles of energy from earlier (see page 14)? Visualise them loaded with context from our words as they are thrust into the universe ready for decoding and response. That little girl I was who didn't feel seen didn't realise how inadvertently powerful she was in making that so. She fought to be seen

Clear Quartz

and then tired of it, meaning each time she pushed to break the call out, she incidentally reinforced it with hows and whys, rather than rewriting the script or the spell. All this to say that the intention behind what is said and how it is said is extremely powerful. When we work on tuning into our intentions, that which we cast out becomes clearer.

Think of casting out like your spiritual Deliveroo app – what's the order? What do you want to eat energetically? What truly feels good? What are you hungry for? And for what reasons? The order is rarely wrong if the intention behind it is clear.

CALL IN

The call in is the energetic momentum at which the response, the manifestation, reaches back to you. You may have cleared the way ready to cast out, but how open is your physical and spiritual front door to believing in the receipt? The call in is the strength of the vibration you are pulling back towards you, it's the smoothness of the line reeling in on a fishing rod – it's the work you do every day answering the call from the universe, feeling into the result before you can see it with your own two human eyes. Two huge parts of calling in are: that which is for your highest good, and our old faithful pal patience…

THE HIGHEST GOOD

Manifesting isn't about having stuff and ownership of people – it's about casting out for and calling in that which is good for you. Or in other words, for your highest good. Sometimes you will have a sense of what that is and sometimes it will be beyond your wildest imaginings. It's like when you eat something that agrees with you, you feel full of goodness and therefore full of life. But when the tummy doesn't agree with what you are digesting, you will sure as anything know about it through a sluggish feeling. I am a cheese lover, but I am beyond intolerant and yet for years I would just eat it because the initial taste was too good to avoid and so I ignored the intelligence of my being. You cannot control your highest good but it is very easy to get caught up in *trying* to control it, or *making* yourself believe that something is 'good' for you (like me with the cheese). It might feed your ego or give you instant gratification or a quick fix: it looks good, in the short term it feels good, and it 'fits' in with what you want. Ultimately though, if the universe deems it no longer serving of your highest good, it will move it on by.

PATIENCE

I've touched on patience already but I'm bringing it back here as repetition and practice is an important part of the process. When fear, worry or impatience sink in, come to

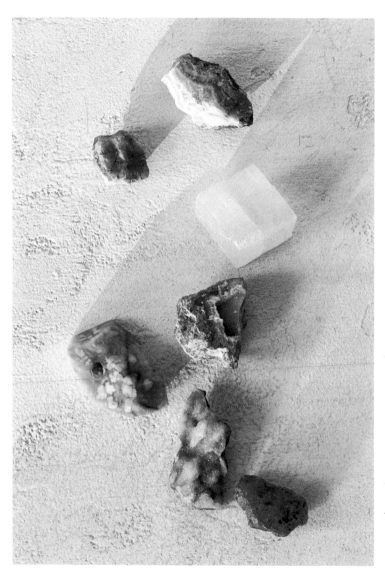

Blue Lace Agate, Carnelian, Optical Calcite, Pink Flower Agate, Spirit Quartz

your crystals, clear the way, set your lens of intention, re-empower your casting out and see how brilliantly clear the way to you is. Remember that what is coming to you needs to come at its own pace before it meets you on the level you have strived so beautifully and brilliantly to create.

THINGS TO KEEP AT HEART & IN MIND AS WE MOVE ON

Before we explore any further, there is a little energy housekeeping to bear in mind. Like does indeed attract like, you are a magnet for miracles – but you need to remember:

- There are some occasions when life brings you a vibration that does not resonate nor vibe with you. You can dismiss it; that's right, you have choice. Just because a vibration arrives, you don't have to rush to call it fate and lump yourself with it if it doesn't feel good.

- Life happens and how we choose to interact with it either brings us growth or gives us another chance to break the habit and find the new.

- Due to old habits, you might feel you aren't able to tell what feels good for you. Fret not, there is a crystal and a practice in here for that.

- When we change, we break away from the 'old' – be that old habits, old beliefs, old lies, loves, friends. These leave an energetical mark that we need to disperse otherwise that mark sits in our energy framework, lives in our aura and creates a shift in our frequency of attraction so that it becomes outdated, or no longer serving of us.

- You are not broken. You can always fine-tune, retune or play another instrument of self – your mind will tell you that you are stuck when you are more free than it'll ever let you know.

- Sometimes we can feel suffocated or squashed, life can be hard and heavy. The energy from the lies we tell ourselves or are told, the disappointment or the pain holds a weight just as powerful as laughter and joy. Fortunately, we can lift it, we can manifest brighter days and better feelings… please know you deserve it.

- You deserve that which is good for you, your mental and physical health.

- Energy is yours for the making and taking… as is life!

- Patience is your dearest, truest teacher and friend. Bring it in… closer.

- Have fun, play in the process – you've got this!

PART 3

GETTING STARTED

Amazonite, Lepidolite

Knowing just how important it is that you are energetically aligned, we arrive at a section you should come back to regularly. I know that you are probably itching to get to the manifesting, but before we get there, I need to take you through three practices that will enable you to use your crystals to clear the way, cast out and call back in.

These practices focus on cleaning, balancing and aligning the energy centres (chakras) in your body, which work to clear out any information, energy or beliefs that no longer serve you. Doing this will turn your entire being into a super manifesting receptor and transmitter.

Golden Healers, Clear Quartz

These are the crystal crew to call on whenever you are ready to change intention, and reinforce or realign one. Come back to these crystals and these practices regularly to work that intuitive muscle and, most importantly, check in on yourself. Read the practice through a few times before you dive in, or better yet record yourself reading it so that you can be guided through it as you do it.

CRYSTAL COLLABORATIONS TO:

CLEAR THE WAY

Align your energies, body and spirit

Time to clear out any energetical blockages to get you ready to manifest. This is the rock squad to support you:

Selenite

Connects to spirit, the universe and all things the other side of the veil. Building communication with 'who' or 'what' you are talking to and strengthening the focus and belief in knowing the message is received.

Pink Tourmaline

A deep cleanse crystal that alleviates old patterns and pathways of pain. It is an angel in releasing grief held within the body. Along with beliefs that are, consciously or subconsciously, shaping your perception energetically, and the way in which you cast out and receive.

Malachite & Rose Quartz

A powerful team. Malachite is the crystal vacuum cleaner for the soul, moving through your being and sucking out with almighty force all that is not serving you, all that energy dust hiding in the corners of self. Coupling this

Malachite, Rose Quartz, Selenite

Pink Flower Agate

with Rose Quartz, the mother of unconditional love, is like pouring a soothing honey-like frequency over the rapid shifts caused by Malachite's powerful cleansing.

PLACEMENT ON THE BODY

Selenite: in between the legs, on the floor or in bed as you sit or lie.

Pink Tourmaline: on or in alignment with the heart centre (middle of chest) or above the top of your head, depending on what feels best to you.

Rose Quartz: in the left hand, palm faced up and open

Malachite: in the right hand, palm faced down and closed.

THE PRACTICE

1 Lay with the crystals in situ, ideally with your body flat on the floor or your bed. Set a timer for a minimum of eight minutes.

2 Take five long breaths in through the nose and out the mouth, closing your eyes when you are ready.

3 Recite the following mantra five times. Let it soothe you, rather than rush you.

    Mantra: May my crystals clear the way, for all that is coming through and rooting all that shall stay.

4   Allow your mind and attention to be drawn to that which of your clearing squad is drawing your awareness towards it, that which is making itself known to you (maybe a pulse, a prickle, a heat, a coolness or simply a knowing.) Check in from Rose Quartz to Malachite, Pink Tourmaline to Selenite; circulate this attention cycle again five times. Using the power of awareness or intention, feel for the weight, the vibe, the heat, the state of the crystal – this is activating the energy between the crystals as a team and with your awareness you are inviting it in deeper into your energy stream.

5   Hover in the energy, witness which crystal piece is resonating with you most today, which is working loudest for you, which feels the punchiest. Any emotions or feelings that rise are being drawn to the surface by your crystals, they will filter that for you – please do not judge it or you, just let it come, let it go, let it be.

6   When the timer rings, blink your eyes open. Remain on the floor or bed for a few breaths, letting what's passed go, and what soothes you to integrate deeper.

7   I always encourage you to write down what came up, what moved through you, either in a journal or in the notes app on your phone (or make use of the voice notes function if verbalising is more your thing). This is just to let you process, to move out what is healing.

8 You can then lay the crystals out in the sun light (arrange them in the same formation) to continue to cleanse through that which has been released from you and also from their energetical being. This will also give them a little more fire for the next 48 hours.

9 When the sun sets, or when the next sun rises – you can separate them out, placing them away from each other in different rooms or spaces in the home. Choose the space that they are drawing you to. Ask yourself what 'looks' or 'feels' good? This is an indicator of where that energy from your shift is living within your home. Placing them within that space allows them to carry on that intentioned work, to continue to filter that energy through the home as much as the self.

10 Please repeat the practice no more than once a week. Go easy on yourself and have fun – shifts and healing don't need to be harsh, full on and constant.

Labradorite, Rainbow Moonstone, Optical Calcite

CRYSTAL COLLABORATIONS TO:

CAST OUT

Knowing what to manifest

How do I know if what I am manifesting is right for me? The answer is as simple as it's in the feeling: if it feels right deep within then it will be. The key is to try and understand what is at the root of your intention. So, rather than manifesting 'a new car', try and think about what that represents. Is it that you are seeking freedom to drive away? Instead of a specific material ask, focus on the desired end goal and try to sit with how that feels to you. That's how we work out if it's something we truly need, rather than just want. So, how exactly do we do that? This is the rock squad to support you:

Rainbow Moonstone

Our ethereal friend who soothes and then packs a healthy punch. A piece that injects a sense of wealth, of energetical richness into our dreams.

Optical Calcite

The heart and aura cleanser – the pattern shifter and the purpose awakener, the lens of knowing.

Labradorite

The reflector of the truth of our hearts; its needs, wants, wishes, its potential and its potency.

YOUR MANIFESTATION LETTER (OR LIST)

We write to the universe as a ritual, as a focal point and a healthy habit. It allows us to get clear with ourselves and keep coming back to check in as to whether something feels relevant to us later or if we need to reset the intention. Are we still clinging to an old goal? Or do we not believe it can ever happen? Getting it down on paper is the first part in the creative practice of energising your being to attract.

Now, you may be someone who has written dozens of letters to the universe or lists with your wants, wishes, desires and needs. You may have burned them or buried them in the soil to transmute them into being. Alternatively, you may be someone who feels uncomfortable asking for anything or may be very new to writing out what you want.

Whichever stage of the game you're in, start fresh with your manifestation letter, which is essentially a top 10 list of things you are ready to bring into your life. You may be wordy, like me, or perhaps you'd like to get to the point and list your wishes in bullet points of one or a few words. I'm going to share how I start my letters to the universe. Wherever you are in your journey, please stick with the structure but always feel free to tweak as you feel you need to. This is a personal practice that allows you to focus on communicating what you are really feeling. Trust your gut and go with it.

Always date your letter, then begin:

Dear Spirit, dear all those who see, please can I ask for your help in supporting me with:

This is where you write your top 10 list. It can be paragraphs or a simple list. Don't worry about specifics, just get it all out and down. Think of it as a spiritual brain dump. When you have finished close your letter with:

Thank you, it is done, it is done, it is done. Yours truly, Me xx

Rainbow Moonstone, Green Aventurine

THE PRACTICE

Please read this entire practice through before starting it, while also asking yourself, 'Am I a morning person (sun-driven) or a night owl (moon-led)?' Each element – the sun and the moon – holds a different energy (fire and water respectively) and our desire for either can change or we can be staunchly dedicated wholly to one. Neither is right nor wrong, just different. Please trust your gut and hold that question for a moment, while we gather our thoughts and our tools.

1   This practice begins with the letter that lists your manifestations – have this to hand.

2   If you are sun-driven please do this in the morning, anytime up until midday. If you are moon-led, start this practice as the sky settles past dusk, even if you can't see the moon, you can sure as anything feel her there.

3   Take your list and read it out loud three times, almost as if you're directing it towards the sun or the moon. Note how this feels. Place your hand on your heart, take three breaths, filling yourself up, then exhale it out into creation.

4　Fold your list up, the intention being that you are letting it sit in that space – that open void or vacuum of potential, potency and creation – bathing it under universal light.

5　Place the list with all three crystals on top of it in a safe place, such as on your windowsill, desk, in a plant pot or flower bed, in or out of your home, to gather the full forces of Mother Nature. Let them sit and bathe under the moonlight if you are moon-led or under sunlight if you are sun-driven.

6　Give yourself some time here, leave the letter under the crystals in situ for as long as is needed – and yes this is also a patience practice: it could be one day, four days, it could be weeks, but come back to that place when you are ready, when you feel instinctively drawn to it or have the time to. Set a reminder, then let it go and let it be.

7　When you're ready, take your crystals off your letter – place your Rainbow Moonstone to your left on your desk or the floor in front of you, and Labradorite to your right. Keep your Optical Calcite and your letter in your hands.

Chrysocolla, Yellow Optical Calcite, Peach Optical Calcite

8 Now lay your letter in-between the two crystals in front of you and take Optical Calcite in your dominant hand. Gently soothe and slide your crystal over the words and sentences one by one on the page. For example, if you have ten manifestations, smooth her over item one, and then come back to draw her over the same item, but this time read every word out loud as it comes from underneath her.

9 As you reach the end of the manifestation or sentence, stop and say out loud 'Reach for or realign' – listen to the resonance in your body, in your being. How does saying those words feel – prickly and in need of release or shift, or warm and toasty and ready to form?

10 Do this for each item on the list, crossing out any that no longer serve you, rewriting any that are a little off key and reaffirm on a new list in a fresh letter with all that feels ready to come home to roost.

11 Always release your old lists as they hold old energies – not just on the paper but in your being. You want to avoid planting seeds for the future on lists that no longer serve you. You can burn them safely in a candle flame (please put it in a large pan) or outside on Mother Earth's soil. Cast the ashes into the wind, bury them or let them swill in water and down and out through the plug hole. Do whichever resonates with you at the time

12 Keep the realigned list with your crystal buddies on it and repeat the practice within a four to six week cycle.

As soon as you have put pen to paper you are manifesting. In fact as soon as you picked up this book you started realigning that which you are working towards or calling in. In becoming more decisive about your wants and needs you are manifesting. Continually reviewing and realigning our manifestations makes the cast out to them even stronger and the calling in much quicker.

The importance of this practice is to keep aligned with the intention of our manifestation. Some of what you are calling out for will be instantly accessible, some will follow at the speed it needs to come. The more you hone in on what you want, what is truly for the highest of your good, the less you will need to spend time revisiting and realigning. Just you watch!

Lepidolite

CRYSTAL COLLABORATIONS TO:

CALL IN

Everyday energisers to draw in your highest good.
Manifestation mantra fuel and, patience practices

You've spent time working out what to manifest – but how can you add energy to your manifestations? How can you make sure you're open to receiving what you've cast out into the universe? We need to allow ourselves to be the everyday beacon of light to direct our manifestations home, like blinking cats' eyes on a runway landing strip. I have eight crystals here that we can align to our seven energy centres and our auric field directly. So that, when we are feeling a little off centre we can work with these crystals to realign, or if we want to stoke the internal fires to allow ourself to burn that bit brighter, we can pour crystal fire lighter energy on them!

With practice, we can simply scan the body and know which crystal can charge us up or clear the way. You can also start to pair and/or mix these crystals with others you already own or other crystals described throughout the book, to help move out your way all that is energetically holding you back and to add more power to the intention you are nurturing. Each crystal correlates to a particular energy centre or chakra, and comes with an intention. Have a read of these before coming to the practice.

Tourmalated Quartz: *the aura*

Citrine: *the crown*

Golden Healer: *the third eye*

Rainbow Fluorite: *the throat*

Tiger's Eye: *the heart*

Hematite: *the solar plexus*

Flower Agate: *the sacrum*

Apatite: *the base*

The Aura: Tourmalated Quartz

— *Aura Intention: I resonate, I receive*
— *Aura colour: white*

The energy field that surrounds our entire being, our aura is like our own personal ozone layer, and just like the earth's protective perimeter, over time toxicity or misalignment causes imbalances or holes in this precious layer. It's super important we tend to this protective shield around us. Tourmalated Quartz is the aura air freshener we all need in our lives, ridding us of negativity in our energy field – it restores, washes and rebalances aura, so we have a strong greenhouse to grow and develop within.

Chakra no. 7: Citrine

— *Crown Intention: I am a sovereign being*
— *Chakra colour: violet*

Sometimes we can confuse understanding what's best with knowing what we *think* is best. Citrine is the stone of flow, allowing thought to be purified, so the intention can be moved more deeply into intuitive thinking and understanding in the manifestation process.

Chakra no. 6: Golden Healer

— *Third Eye Intention: I see, I glow*
— *Chakra colour: indigo*

Tension in the eyes can make life appear grey – so let's get golden. These beauties allow the way in which we see the world through both our actual and our mind's eyes to resonate on high velocity, to give clarity to the truth of what is actually before you, rather than what you think you already know to be there.

Chakra no. 5: Rainbow Fluorite

— *Throat Intention: I speak, I show*
— *Chakra colour: blue*

Our words become our way, it's true! Rainbow Fluorite allows the flow of communication to be created in accordance with your highest potential. It will take you up high, above the waves of your words as you have previously known them, so you can communicate clearly between self and spirit, the universe and those around you – bringing clarity and trust in your voice of creation.

Tiger's Eye

Chakra no. 4: Tiger's Eye

— *Heart Intention: I love, I become*
— *Chakra colour: green*

I believe we all need the confidence to love, to understand our love, how we love and how we wish to be loved. Tiger's Eye gives our heart the confidence in its purest ability, to move, to be and to soar without wavering. It will raise you above any doubt you may hold about how you embody love.

Chakra no. 3: Hematite

— *Solar Plexus Intention: I do, I know*
— *Chakra colour: yellow*

I love Hematite, he's a magnetic force to be reckoned with. In this day and age, it is often our inner selves that can feel most punched when things don't appear to sway in our favour, or when we give and give of ourselves without asking for much back. A magnetic support to bring in the right forces is what we all need here. Let it come to you, yes, but let's use some crystal punch and positive force!

Chakra no. 2: Flower Agate

— *Sacral Intention: I feel, I flow*
— *Chakra colour: orange*

This is an energetic space of emotional storage, energy can flow from here or stagnate. I like to use crystals to allow that which has passed to transform into a manner that allows the new and the healthy to flourish from within you – Flower Agate grounds the past and blooms the heart-led truth of the new.

Chakra no. 1: Apatite

— *Base Intention: I am, I can*
— *Chakra colour: red*

This is the space of fruition. It's not just about knowing who you are, it's about knowing you are part of it all. Honouring that space within us makes us understand our true worth and the fact that we deserve access to 'it all'. Apatite connects us from above, to below. She will deepen your connection and your alignment to you and your part in the bigger picture and the bounty that flows from that.

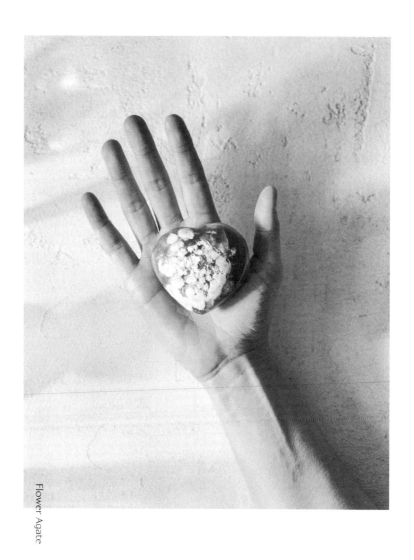

Flower Agate

THE PRACTICE

There are a few ways to work with these pieces and their corresponding centres – go with what suits your needs and the time you have available to you. (Although I urge you to give yourself permission to play with them all.)

1 Scan the list or the picture on page 57, and decide which crystal is calling to you and use it in your regular meditation practice.

Or

2 If you don't have a regular mediation practice:

i. Scan the words or the image that calls to you – which are you most drawn to?

ii. Sit comfortably, cross legged on floor with you back against wall or hard surface for support, or sit on a chair, your feet flat against the floor.

iii. Set a timer on your phone (let's use tech in a positive fashion where we can) for a minimum of five minutes (in time you can expand the length).

iv. Place the crystal of intuitive choice in your left hand, palm facing up and resting on your knee – the energy centre of this hand feeds the energy directly into heart.

v. Take three long cleansing breathes in through the nose and out through the mouth. Close your eyes if and when that feels comfortable to you. If you would rather your eyes remain open, then keep your gaze on the crystal in your hand.

vi. You can direct this flow of healing, enlightening energy from the heart to the corresponding energy centre, by very simply reciting over and over the correlating intention until the timer sings. Do this whilst bringing all your attention to the corresponding energy centre, allowing it to move from there to the crystal and to allow you to feel in that flow.

vii. When thought tries to break your focus be kind to it and move back to the mantra, focus your vision on the feeling of the crystal.

viii. When the timer sings, let the intention, your focus, all go and just be in that moment, in that energy. Take notice of what comes to or from you – be that a feeling, a warmth or a visual, write it down when you are ready (and only when you are ready).

Or

3   Take your crystal(s) to the bath – that's right, water
     amplifies the vibration. Run a bath with salt (Himalayan
     or Epsom) as a cleanser of your energies and put the
     crystal in with you. Just by sitting in the water she will
     pulse her cleaning properties in and through you. If you
     are using Rainbow Flourite, please place her by the side
     of the bath because she is porous and just as effective
     outside the water. Use this as a space to visualise,
     daydream, feel into and play with your manifestations.
     There should be no pressure, let that which needs to shift
     be shifted by the water and the crystal lift your vision,
     pulling in powers on high.

Or

4   Take them to bed – sleep time is so effective for nurturing
     our intentions and manifestations, and for tending to the
     soothing of our energies. We can often, I believe, take
     the messaging from our dreams for granted. It's a time
     where much is revealed and much planted. Imagine the
     power of your crystal holding you rock steady while your
     mind shifts and reveals in your sleep. I like to keep a
     notebook to the side of my bed to channel out all that I
     remember of what was revealed in sleep. You can then
     refer back to see if this needs to be cleared, cast out or
     called in.

67

Tourmalated Quartz, Citrine, Golden Healer, Rainbow Fluorite, Tiger's Eye, Hematite, Flower Agate, Apatite

Selenite

CRYSTALS
TO MANIFEST
THE SPECIFICS

ACROSS
YOUR LIFE

The heavenly crystals laid out in this section have been curated to support you in clearing, casting out and calling in, across various aspects of your life – whether you are looking to manifest more confidence, greater communication, deeper love of self, supporting family or your furry friends. I believe that crystals call to you and work uniquely with you, so I've made sure that there are different choices of crystals for each topic, depending on what you connect with.

Pink Tourmaline, Pink Flower Agate

DEEPENING YOUR CRYSTAL CONNNECTION

You will see that each piece has a mantra alongside it to help you deepen your connection with your crystals. Remember, crystals love to be given a job, love to be busy, love a direction, so when you pick your crystal for the scenario you are manifesting, take time to sit with it. Don't be afraid to ask of it, explain to it, as if talking to a friend, the space in which you find yourself in life right now and what you would like them to help you call in or clear out your way. Once you have communicated your need, take the crystal to hand, close your eyes and breathe in three cleansing breaths (in through the nose out through the mouth) before reciting the mantra three times. You can also use them within one of the practices in part three. Where there are crystals that would work particularly well with one of these practices, I have included a note. As always though, trust yourself and lean in to what feels good. For the group crystal practices, you can swap crystals that correlate with either the crystal or the chakra colour.

Anything goes, play, enjoy, make it a way to uplift your everyday rather than being a bore or a chore. The mantras will allow you to tap into the energy, the flow of that crystal at any time of day, wherever you find yourself, even if you have left your piece at home! Fret not, for you can call in on their energy from afar.

Lepidolite

MANIFESTING THE SELF

Manifesting who we are is a hugely important part of our life's journey. Creating and honouring who we are happens with every thought and interaction, and this process can be made so much easier when working with crystals and their divine frequencies. To keep the body and being in a clear state of receptivity is like adding the base paint to your walls at home – once that is laid and smoothed, you can add any colour and change that colour at any time. When we choose to honour our energy, and when we naturally manifest the self, we truly understand that manifesting isn't about having things or people, nor about ownership. It is about being in a state of pure receptivity. These next crystal edits are all about and for you...

Blue Amethyst
FOR SELF-LOVE

Self-love comes as a manifestation of self-honouring – when you are no longer needing to fight against what or who you are, nor needing to fight for the world to believe who you are or 'buy into' you. Blue Amethyst is a shield, or comforting cloak. It allows us to be held strong as he works towards dissipating the perceptions we find painful to carry, helping us work to replace them with positive and true intention and reflection.

Mantra: I release the fight, I draw in the love and bliss.
Other crystals: Garnet, Rose Quartz
Practice: Cast out

Lepidolite
FOR TRANSFORMING WORRY IN TO WORTH

Worry is seemingly a default setting but it leads us into the unknown with unstable footing, causing us to feel blind as to where we are going and how. Lepidolite holds a frequency that stabalises your being, allowing you to walk in emotional balance into the unknown. Let Lepidolite ease the worry and re-form it, giving you the confidence to look into the unknown with bravery, wisdom and excitement.

Mantra: I am transforming every day, who I am is worth all I am creating.
Other crystals: Snowy Quartz, Green Opal
Practice: Clear the way, Cast out, Call in

Orange Calcite
FOR GOOD VIBRATIONS

Manifesting sunlight and good vibrations into and around your life is an inside job. We could all use Orange Calcite and her radiant glow in our life to create more of that good feeling. Orange Calcite drops her essence into the fire of our being deep at the belly – constantly restoring the energy of our heart – ensuring that, just like the sun, we continue to rise and we never burn out.

Mantra: I am restored, restoring, reigniting.
Other crystals: Pyrite
Practice: Call in

Blue & Orange Calcite

Apatite
FOR POSITIVE REFLECTIONS

Clearing the way, as we know, is super important. One of the keys to being in a divine state of manifestation is knowing that all you see around you (in life, in others) reflects that which you are, and that which you decide who you are. Apatite allows us to do many a thing with our sight, she clears the vision, she holds the truth, she expands our knowledge of self and the world around us – which in turn allows us to work on reflecting our true self into the world.

Mantra: I am that which I see – what I see resonates highly and clearly for me.
Other crystals: Iolite, Snowy Quartz, Labradorite
Practice: Clear the way, Cast out

Turquoise
FOR BECOMING

You don't need to stand on the edge of your picture, being the supporting role. You are becoming, manifesting the self and doing it beautifully, so please allow Turquoise, like the magical spider she is, to weave all that you are becoming into your being and out into the universal web in the sky. So, you can cast those signals in complete empowerment of self, knowing you are hand in hand weaving the way.

Mantra: I weave my way, each and every day.
Other crystals: Larimar, Sodalite, Hematite
Practice: Call in

Dalmatian Stone Jasper & Tiger's Eye
FOR TRUST & CONFIDENCE

You have been burned – you have asked, believed and not received or perhaps you have received and it didn't land as you felt it might. So how do you get past the worry of it not working out again? When you are ready to call back to you all the energy you sent out from past intentions that ended in disappointment, allow Dalmatian Stone Jasper to help you repurpose that energy back into trust. Then hand over to Tiger's Eye to turn the key back on your confidence drive to trust once more in spirit, in the universe, in yourself, in the 'unreal', and in the process of the journey and the ways in which they deliver. Together this power pair will also connect you to your higher self, reminding you of what feels good (your highest good), what should remain and equally that which you have attracted that no longer resonates with you. They will also allow some space for that expectation of the unexpected!

Mantra: I allow myself to release what has passed and have faith in what is.

Other crystals: Rainbow Moonstone & Dalmatian Stone Jasper, Optical Calcite & Rainbow Fluorite

Dalmatian Stone Jasper

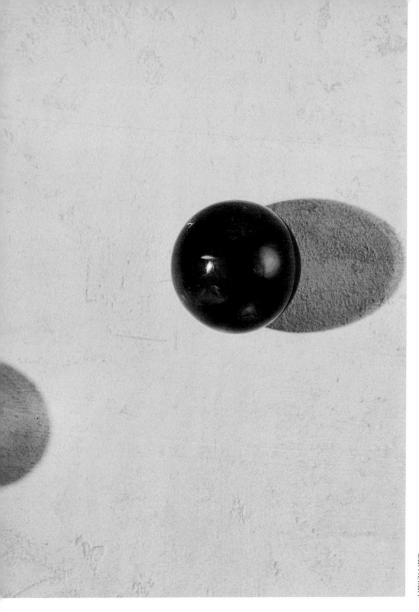

Carnelian & Green Opal
FOR MANIFESTING YOUR GLOW

We can indeed manifest healthy cells, vitality and high energy without creating an unintentional burnout. This is a pairing I have been playing a lot with of late and would love for you to take to hand. On her own, Carnelian allows us and our energy to bounce without force, gives us a spring in our step including on heavier days when even the coffee doesn't kick it. Green Opal allows us to cleanse out, supporting all systems of our being in getting them up to their optimum. As a team, Carnelian lifts up the rug of self us Green Opal clears out all the dust. No covering up, no quick fixes, glowing at your optimum is the only way these pair know how.

Mantra: The glow is real, the glow is mine.
Other crystals: Malachite & Rose Quartz, Tourmalated Quartz & Black Tourmaline

Sunstone
FOR BREAKTHROUGH ENERGY FLOW

Just as plants need the sun to trigger their blooming, sometimes so do we. Often we have knowingly set about healing the self and planted many a brilliant seed – but the sunlight or the conditions for that blooming have yet to show. Sunstone, as per her affectionate namesake, cracks through the hard layers we have implemented in preservation to get to the seed to create miracles and magic without the mind needing to dive deep. Time to light the way and allow that which you have been tending to come into its fullest fruition.

Mantra: I am breaking through the barrier of self – to fully allow the fruition of me.
Other Crystals: Pyrite, Trolleite, Pink Flower Agate
Practice: Clear the way, Call in

Black Obsidian, Fire Agate, Labradorite

Trolleite
FOR THE ART OF RECEIVING

Trolleite is a restful awakener – a crystal that allows you to ground into the here and now whilst letting your spirit, your essence, fly creatively sky-high. A piece to allow you to blend your reality into the waking day and to feel it, feel what you are creating, casting out for – to feel it before it lands ready. Are you ready to receive? You are now!

Mantra: I am ready, willing, open and receiving.
Other crystals: Lepidolite, Citrine, Aura Quartz
Practice: Call in

Black Onyx, Selenite & Rose Quartz
FOR PERSONAL SPACE

You can't truly escape life, we try to run from it, but we can't – not really – we just step out of a vibe for a brief moment and then dive straight back into it. To actively promote change and create a sacred space away from what may feel like heavy or dense energy from others we need to create a personal energy hotspot. Black Onyx draws up from the roots of Mother Earth a grounding umbrella, dispelling unserving vibrations – rooting down the electrical storm that has been brewing, into the extinguishing earth. The Selenite creates a heavenly bubble around your entity. The Rose Quartz allows you to hold compassion, loving focus, to be in your frustrations or just sit in your own space to recharge, recreate, reexamine, reconnect, refocus. I place these around my work space, it's the room I probably spend most time in and the space most people move in and out of. Try where feels best but my recommendation would be to place the pieces in alignment with their correlating energy. So Black Onyx will sit resplendently on the ground, the Selenite, as best you can, on a level in alignment or above your head and place Rose Quartz bed-side, desk-level or, of course, on your person. Have fun with this one. Open the space and you will never need to run from home again, you will be able to melt and recharge in the comfort of your own heavenly nest.

Mantra: I am home and at ease always in my entire being. May I allow it to be nurtured, calm, clear and clean.
Other crystals: Tourmaline, Scolecite, Rhodonite

Charoite

MANIFESTING LOVE

Love comes in a bounty of shapes, sizes, textures and scales, and that sheer amount of choice can often overwhelm us. We reach often for what's there rather than tuning into that which really is of our vibe. We can be over-giving, under believing of receiving this beautiful fuel of love – but it is for EVERYONE, made by everyone – it is the energy of all things. We have the power and ability to harness and effect the flow of that vibration in every area of our lives. With our crystal companions we can release habits and unlock doors.

Charoite
FOR UNCONDITIONAL LOVE & BLISS

Unconditional love breeds self-worth and makes us the magnet of loving and bliss. It also makes us energetically hyper-attractive – a happy problem right? But I believe unconditional love is our birth right and charoite can help you take that right by the hand. Charoite is also a piece we can use to transform all battle wounds of love, restore you to power, back to creative, passionate play. Ready to find out what love really has got to do with it? This is your forever soulmate stone.

Mantra: Love and bliss – I was born for this.
Other crystals: Pink Kunzite, Rhodonite, Rose Quartz
Practice: Call in

Pink Kunzite
FOR MANIFESTING ROMANCE

Ooh what a beauty Pink Kunzite is! She puts the heart back into a relationship or your belief in love and romance, and most importantly into you. If you are ready for romance or to re-spark the flame then Pink Kunzite is the kindling, the charcoal and the flame. She is a super transformer when it comes to love, connecting you to how you truly deserve to be loved and romanced whilst burning outdated beliefs and experiences. Allow her to move your vibe to the origins of your heart energy, working with you to show you how yours truly wants and deserves to be romanced and loved.

Mantra: In through the eye of my heart – love is awakened, romance reborn.
Other crystals: Aventurine, Pink Tourmaline, Pink Opal
Practice: Cast out, Call in

Pink Kunzite

Amethyst Spirit Quartz & Fire Quartz
FOR CALLING THEM IN

Your partner, your teammate, your soulmate, however you term it, they – that beautiful being – just like your beautiful being, is an energy, a light. You are both worthy of bringing your beings together and creating one mega orbit. Calling out to your heart's connection is a scary one – it can be full of doubt and worry, that's why this power pair are the rock squad you need to anchor yourself to at this time. Fire Quartz blasts through and tends to the mental anxiety of past relationships, gently alchemising the fear and doubt back into your natural abundant bounce. Whilst the Amethyst Spirit Quartz lets you call out your desires, needs, beliefs at your frequency – your vibrational channel. The clear energy chimney created by the Fire Quartz heightens your call, making it clear and real only for those who are worthy to hear it and feel the power of your love.

Mantra: From my heart to yours I call – ready to love, to be, to evolve.

Other crystals: Pink Tourmaline & Dalmatian Stone Jasper, Blue Calcite & Selenite

MANIFESTING FOR FAMILY & FRIENDS
(INCLUDING THE FURRY ONES)

Rhodochrosite
FOR FAMILY LOVE

Sometimes the focus can become so big, so wide, we become fearful we don't have enough to give to those we love around us. The family is a wonderful matrix, it can be a complicated, confused one or a joyful and lighthearted one. Keeping the love here alive and flowing comes from a space of acceptance. Working with Rhodochrosite allows us to accept every individual in our tribe for exactly who and what they are. It allows us to see who they can become and allows us to send and radiate energy and love their way.

Mantra: To my family, for my tribe – may our hearts be open and our dreams cast wide.
Other crystals: Ocean Jasper, White Jade, Green Calcite, Carnelian
Practice: Call in

Rhodochrosite

Blue Lace Agate

Blue Lace Agate & Green or Pink Flower Agate
FOR THE KIDS

It's important we learn to give our kids the energy they need to manifest the greatest versions of themselves and their reality, whilst being sure not to deplete from our own flow and direction. Blue Lace Agate allows our brilliant miniatures to tap into the power of communication, allowing them to express their own dreams, wishes and manifestation magic without you needing to plant it for them. The Green or Pink Flower Agate both sing to allowing the true essence of self to bloom, to manifest through energetical nurture. Let kids play with them, host them in their rooms – let your babies show you the way, kids are wonderfully intuitive in the pureness of their essence. Make the flow of life fun not forced!

Mantra: Through child-like wonder and play I see the magic of manifestation in each and every day.
Other crystals: Green Agate, Lapis Lazuli, Sodalite
Practice: Cast out, Call in

Dalmatian Stone Jasper & Rose Quartz
FOR LOVING YOUR FRIENDS

This crystal collaboration allows us to create healthy parameters, rather than building walls and boundaries which in time only manifest pain, hurt and often anger. Working with the crystal that upholds all that it means to be loyal within us, Dalmatian Stone Jasper, allows us to attract all those who are loyal to us. Let the Rose Quartz soothe anything in our friendships that bristles against our being and values, so we can stand in love with each other as we need to serve you both.

Mantra: To my friend and for the friend in me – loving, healthy parameters I set for you and me.
Other crystals: Amazonite & Amethyst, Howlite & Jade
Practice: Cast out

Clear Quartz & Rose Quartz
FOR UNTANGLING ENERGY

As we learn to understand what is ours energetically – we need to clear connections, ties and bonds that hold us back or that we have outgrown. This power pair allows us to clean up and manifest healthy energy in ALL our relationships, all our connections. Clear Quartz is the master swordsman, who slices though the b*llsh*t, all the vibrational chords that no longer or never did serve or sing to the vibe we wish to ride. Rose Quartz soothes the flow, sending new life and growth to connections in need of regeneration or laying to rest those which have flown.

Mantra: I am untangled, free to flow, taking with me all that helps me grow.
Other crystals: Clear Quartz & Rhodonite, Ametrine & Citrine
Practice: Clear the way

Kyanite & Clear Quartz
ALL THE VIBES UNDER ONE ROOF

That which vibes right for me is not necessarily right for you. So, how do we navigate the energies in the home when we have so many synergies, but also so many potential clashes? To 'try to balance' sounds exhausting, right? We clear and honour everyone's energy and we use Kyanite to take on that task, to filter that which is good to the rightful owner. A super smart, sophisticated and steady crystal, I would suggest purchasing one piece to represent each being (including your fluffy friends!) that reside under the one roof. Clear Quartz comes in then as our master flow stone – bringing source energy to fuel the whole house in their ambitions, dreams and manifestations. I would suggest placing a Kyanite piece in each person's room and the Quartz in the heart of the home, which tends to be the living room or kitchen (feel what is best for you!). Another option is to place the pieces of Kyanite pointing towards the Clear Quartz. The Clear Quartz will kick to each individual, sharing the vibes, filtering and lifting the united front!

Mantra: May we all rise and flow for one and as one.
Other crystals: Malachite & Rose Quartz, Pink Tourmaline & Aventurine

Blue Kyanite

Green Aventurine
FOR YOUR FUR BABIES

Pets are super beings, angels sent to teach and guide us. They are wonderfully empathetic, they sponge our energy and they respond incredibly to crystals. What I have learned from my pooch Dolly is that they really know energetically what they want. As such, I was given Green Aventurine as our master cheerleader for the animal squad. It is a powerhouse renewing stone, and will renew and revitalise their energy, bring them protection and comfort in spaces where they may feel off-key or off-guard. Green Aventurine will ensure our fears don't get soaked into their being and reflected back to us, allowing our fur friends to teach us the purest lessons without it being at a loss or cost to them. I place pieces in a circle in front of Dolly and she will pick up what she needs or I lay them in a line and she will nestle or grab for what she needs. Please make sure you use larger polished pieces that cannot be swallowed or easily chewed, Selenite in wand form is a huge no as, once in their grip, it will start to break down and down into a million pieces.

Mantra: May I bless my friend with the energy they bless upon me.
Other crystals: Tiger's Eye, Bumble Bee Jasper, Black Tourmaline

Citrine

MANIFESTING FOR ABUNDANCE

Abundance is more than just cash and different expressions of that form. Remember that it is 'the stuff' that hooks us, that we cling to and come to fear, and fear, my friends, really funks with our flow. Abundance is the channel of pure attraction, when your channels are clear it's much easier to be in your highest, purest flow and therefore it's easier for flow to find you. The greatest frustration we have as humans is the need, or the lack that comes and clogs the channels. So, this is a section dedicated to your flow, allowing you to honour and harness all that is for your highest good, from the clearest channel of receptive flow.

Citrine & Green Aventurine
FOR FREEDOM IN FINANCIAL FLOW

Our finances are important, it would be super flippant of me to say grab these stellar pieces and all your worries will be resolved. But what I can tell you is, they can move you into the vibration of excellence, work with you to sustain, maintain and draw home flow, and in turn call the cash to you however the universe sees fit to deliver it. Citrine is perhaps the ultimate stone of flow, she can draw a flow of quite literally anything to you. She's a super hard worker – alleviating panic, worry and moving your awareness in to the true catalyst of conversion for financial flow. Green Aventurine calls to you the opportunities, the hows, the wheres. Let them both teach you and make you feel worthy. You do deserve it, even when experience has taught otherwise.

Mantra: I allow pressure of all form to alleviate and the river of abundance to flow to and from me.

Other crystals: Orange Calcite & Clear Quartz, Jade & Pyrite

Practice: Cast out, Call in

Pyrite
FEELING FOR THE TREASURE

In order to truly manifest, we have to let go of the way in which the mind perceives it *should* look. Don't get me wrong, visualisation is super important – but often it is the way we are looking for something EXACTLY that causes us to miss that which is meant for us when it walks right up to our front door and rings the bell. Pyrite is pure fire, protective rather than destructive. Abundance flow is a channel, and Pyrite burns through the channel with protective grace, eliminating any ego traps or spiritual trips that focus us on the want. In order to truly find treasure you have to seek the feeling rather than seek

Pyrite

Labradorite, Orange Calcite, Lemon Chrysoprase

the map – let the fire of Pyrite light the way and guide the feelings to you, so no opportunity that lands at your door will ever go amiss.

Mantra: I believe and then I see.
Other crystals: Pink Tourmaline, Bloodstone, Jade
Practice: Clear the way

Lemon Calcite
FOR RIDING THE WAVE THAT KEEPS ON GIVING

Flow can often come in waves, but stopping and starting becomes jarring, demotivating and uninspiring so we need a crystal surfboard we can work with to ride that wave and flow. Lemon Calcite is the ultimate energiser who helps turn tests of patience into fun-filled adventures rather than soul-sucking vibes. Allow Lemon Calcite to work with you to find the wave, ride it and move to the next without exhausting or bumming yourself out.

Mantra: I ride the energy waves of life and the currents call all that is needed to me.
Other crystals: Chalcedony, Rainbow Fluorite, Citrine
Practice: Call in

MANIFESTING YOUR POWER & PURPOSE

Our purpose and life's work is made up of many roles – this section is therefore super relevant to us all, be it power and purpose in our career, or in our role as a parent, a partner, etc. Whether you are a super-mum or super-exec or both, each plays a huge part in the tapestry of our manifested life and these roles we have chosen impact all areas of our being and happiness. How we show up to these roles is of course very important, but what's more so is that we get what we need from these roles we play. If we lose sight of our power and purpose we risk swimming in unfulfillment, forgetting that we have the potential to craft the next role in our life or career. Nothing is helpless when it is all in our hands. So time to take your rock squad to show you the way and the how, to move the stickiness, and reignite the fire and drive.

Amazonite
I GOT THE POWER

Taking back your power comes from recognising it within. Sometimes, though we have given so much, it's hard to see our power or feel brave enough to own it and that puts us into a tricky state when we are looking to receive – for we don't believe we have the power to bring it in, or that we deserve to own it. Amazonite fuels us, refills us from where we have given of ourselves too readily. She shows us where we leak our essence into the wants, desires and needs of others. Amazonite works with us to rid anything from our life that seemingly takes our power away – it moves the focus to your true nature, attracting all that supports it.

Mantra: The power is and always was in my hands – we make it and take it so.
Other crystals: Lepidolite, Labradorite, Pyrite, Hematite
Practice: Clear the way, Call in

Celestite
FOR TAPPING INTO PASSION & PURPOSE

We often and easily confuse our work, our job – be that our career or another role in the home – with our passion and purpose. These can of course lead us to our career path, but they're not one and the same. Let Celestite remove the sleepy cloud of life conditioning that tucks you into a set of habits. Let her reveal to you, reawaken you from the perception of deep slumber. Her peace will connect you to the great architect in the sky, delivering and showing you in thought and feeling, through repetitive signs that awaken you back to what you have always known about yourself to be true – that which truly sets your heart on fire, so you can shape, honour and own your purpose.

Mantra: It is known, it is shown – passion, purpose leading me home.
Other crystals: Bloodstone, Clear Quartz, Yellow Calcite, Fire Agate
Practice: Cast out

Celestite

Apophyllite
FOR MAKING & TAKING THE CHANGE

Often we try to manifest a job or a career when we are coming from the wrong angle, and we see the situation as more complex than perhaps it needs to be. Perhaps we fell into the current job, perhaps we chose it and are scared to admit we outgrew it or that we are ready to take on more of a challenge, or take on less! Apophyllite is a truly beautiful stone. It holds a sacred wisdom that shows us with pure transparency (without the feeling of fear or pain) that which we are afraid to admit, allowing it to dissipate. This means you can work with her to see and create the way ahead all at a pace that is pushing you firmly out the comfort zone.

Apophyllite

Mantra: I have the wisdom, the power to see who I am and where I am meant to be.
Other crystals: Trolleite, Optical Calcite, Iolite
Practice: Clear the way, Cast out, Call in

Chrysocolla
FOR REALIGNING THE PATH

What's your truth? It's an amalgamation of experiences, stories and emotions, all working together to direct, to manifest, your next move. We need to come to reset our inner compass back to our true intuitive north star. Sounds like a big job (it can feel like it too), but coming to your truth to manifest the way forward needs the right energetic attention, and Chrysocolla will direct you back towards speaking your truth. Just touching her unlocks this potential within her and directs towards you the reset you've been waiting or fighting for. Let her put the smile back on your face.

Mantra: I realign my heart's compass back to my truth with effortless knowing and ease.
Other crystals: Ruby, Clear Quartz, Sunstone
Practice: Clear the way

Labradorite
FOR STANDING OUT, SHINING YOUR LIGHT & RADIATING YOUR VIBE

Socially it can be frowned upon to peacock yourself about but really it's all in the way you do it. If you are casting out from insecurity or want it is received as such by your audience, whoever they may be. If you shine your little heart out from a space of authentic self, it is felt, and understood. Labradorite is a classic for allowing your heart's truth to shine from your core out into the world in a powerful manner. It teaches us that this isn't selfish or wrong, that being in your light – shining, standing out as and for who you are – is what you were sent here to do.

Mantra: When I shine in my true light, I allow others to shine theirs alongside me.
Other crystals: Jade, Amethyst, Selenite, Fuchsite
Practice: Cast out

Black Obsidian
FOR PHYSICAL & MENTAL DETOXIFICATION

Our crystal collective is constantly clearing the way for us and drawing in for us. When it comes to focusing on our power or our purpose, we can deflate quicker than a whoopee cushion – so we need to detox rather than be deterred. Obsidian is yummy. It's like the shiny night sky, its depths know no bounds. Its potent elixir draws from our depths the internal and auric space junk into its black hole and just like that, it's gone!

Mantra: I effortlessly release all that is intoxicating me.
Other crystals: Garnet, Peridot, Rutilated Quartz
Practice: Clear the way

Black Obsidian

Crazy Lace Agate

MANIFESTING PLAY IN EXTREME CONDITIONS

The clearer our energy gets, the more the gig of life gets real, the more we are aware of our energy, the more conscious we are of spending it wisely. We can also find the more clear our energy, the more lagging we can feel the day after being in denser energy.

This is your crystal crew to manifest clear energy and, if you like hiding in, then they will entice you out. They will connect you with your tribe, soothe your energy if you've been burning too brightly for the world to see and you need to reboot. Or if you need to settle the body in a harmonic state after it's been locked habitually in that state of being.

Crazy Lace Agate
FOR LETTING GO & TAKING THE FUN

When I purchased my Crazy Lace Agate, Barry at The Astrology Store in Covent Garden said to me with a cheeky laugh, 'Be careful with that one, she does exactly as she says on the box', and he was not wrong. This is a magical piece, for the crazy in the title is about letting go, getting beyond the mind rather than losing it, drawing in and manifesting fun into your life with a healthy fizz and natural high and without any hangover – bonus! I would say use for short periods of time – longer may prove quite wiring. Similarly, and perhaps to avoid using at sleep time, unless you want to go disco in your dreams!

Mantra: I let go as I lean into the good times.
Other crystals: Peridot, Moss Agate, Yellow Calcite, Amazonite
Practice: Cast out, Call in

Lapis Lazuli & Yellow Topaz
FOR HEIGHTENED CONNECTIONS

Our tribes can come in all shapes and sizes. Having different social orbits is super normal as it allows your energy to be as it is, a multi-sphere of beaming light. This next power combo brings a magical uplift to our current connections as well as drawing you towards and into connections of a life-affirming level. Lapis Lazuli is the super stone of communication and connection, allowing all our language to sing to our truest, highest frequency – be that verbal, body or energy language. Lapis lights us up, throws our energy arms out wide with specific purpose – reaching that which resonates with us

Lapis Lazuli

Rose Quartz

to the depths of our souls. It goes beyond the surface chitter-chatter, but to those soul connections our heart yearns for. The Yellow Topaz calls you out of your hiding hole and your old habits, lighting the way. It makes the path to your people and yourself alluring, attractive and tantalising, rather than heavy and dragging! This power pair will only allow you to be seen by those with a sharp eye, offering a depth of knowing you are ready for.

Mantra: I cast out for all that is of my level to call in.
Other crystals: Bumble Bee Jasper & Blue Lace Agate, Yellow Calcite & Caribbean Calcite

Rose Quartz, Amethyst & Amazonite
FOR SOCIAL COMFORT

When we step out of the house, no matter how in groove we are with our energies, we have to allow ourselves to step through or brush past another person or place's vibe. Consider all the layers of you being squashed into a bar, cinema or restaurant – under that one roof you could be with say ten, twenty, fifty-plus other beings, just like you but on their own vibe, their own energies. That's between one–fifty other energies to be sensitive of, one–fifty energies in or out of balance; mixing, swirling all in your sweet space. Now, this isn't about heavy duty seal-me-in protection. It's about allowing your energy to be in its own space, while having compassion for another's energy and its condition without holding any of their lower or heavy vibrations close to heart. It's about allowing yourself to enjoy yourself in all energy weather conditions. To do this we bring together a trio of trusted crystal colleagues to help us remain comforted, playful and bright. Rose Quartz will forever be the navigator of the heart allowing us to be soft in hardened situations, rather than softening to soothe the hard in others around us – there is a mega difference in these states! The Amethyst works with us to keep our light and head up – to look through and navigate the space of most comfort for us, the Amazonite allows us to play with the energies, to watch and feel the vibes without carrying them. It also sends off the signal to your people, or those on your frequency, alerting them that you are there – so instead of hunting them out or hiding away until you feel 'safe' you will be manifesting them towards you. This is also a great tribe if you are worried about bumping into an old friend or an ex, or anything the mind is triggering the being into wobbling at – let this trio stabilise you with effortless ease.

Mantra: I am powerful, vibing bright, gently being.
Other crystals: Tiger's Eye, Citrine, Crazy Lace Agate, Smoky Quartz, Rhodochrosite, Optical Calcite

Moss Agate
FOR BALANCE

The crystal of tranquility, Moss Agate brings us back to balance when we have been in one extreme or another, or when we have been in or at play with someone whose energy is a little off kilter. Anytime things have felt extreme or we ourselves have shown extreme behaviour, for example around food, alcohol or negative thinking, Moss Agate is the one that will soothe you emotionally, mentally and physically back to being – back to centre, back to your natural bliss.

Mantra: I effortlessly release all that is intoxicating me.
Other crystals: Rose Quartz, Hematite, Smoky Quartz, Optical Calcite, Pink Tourmaline
Practice: Call in

Clear Quartz

MANIFESTING THROUGH & BEYOND

Life happens, we can't stop it. And when we feel 'broken' in the face of grief and loss, it can be the hardest time to have belief and to hold our faith. At these times, we often don't recognise the metaphorical hole we've sunk into and sometimes part of the process requires we spend some time in its grasp. These support stars are for when the sh*t does hit the proverbial fan. They're here for when you feel raw, to move you through with grace. It's not about escaping or denying the experience but to allow you to start to understand, to gain strength or forgiveness, or whatever it is you need at this time – connecting you to your innate grace and lifting your heart steadily and slowly back into life.

Howlite & Rose Quartz
FOR LOSS

Loss comes in many forms, each experience similar yet incomparable. It's a time when we require pairings of crystals, one to soothe the pain, the other to lovingly and gently lift the heart. Howlite holds us, allows us to touch the somewhat harder emotions found in our loss,

Red Jasper, Moss Agate, Howlite, Clear Quartz

the anger in the hows and whys. Allow Howlite to touch your heart and begin to alleviate the burning within you as her loyal teammate Rose Quartz gently tends with love to the pain within the dense structures of the mind. Squeeze these pieces in your hand when you feel full on any level and they can gently pull the waves of the internal tsunami into a semblance of balance as you make the time to heal.

Mantra: I allow myself to be and move beyond.
Other crystals: Malachite & Rose Quartz, Pink Tourmaline & Apatite, Aquamarine & Jade
Practice: Clear the way

Apache Tear & Strawberry Quartz
FOR NAVIGATING GRIEF

There is no one way of travel when it comes to grief. Apache Tear is the strongest support stone I know, allowing us to stand as best we can in times and winds of change, in times of sorrow. It allows us to remember how to keep going, when our entirety says we surely cannot. Strawberry Quartz places the hands of love around the heart allowing the pain to surface in as gentle a way as possible. Together they give us the strength to stand tall in the storm and put the heart in a space where it can start to see beyond the rain.

Mantra: I am and I can.
Other crystals: Apache Tear & Chrysocolla, Angelite & Apophyllite, Rhodochrosite & Obsidian
Practice: Call in

Blue Calcite & Clear Quartz
WHEN FEELING DISCONNECTED

It's not just the universe or life we can feel disconnected from – but also from ourselves. This is a time we get really into the questioning mind, doubting every thought and feeling of the heart. At this time we work with Blue Calcite, who reminds us that the connection is never truly lost, that you are not lost. Last, she whispers creatively and calmly to your soul and your true essence starts to soften the barriers created, shining light on that which needs regulating and releasing. This in turn directs Clear Quartz to blast out what is truly standing in your way, before allowing you to take back, calmly, your own reigns of self.

Mantra: I release all that holds me back from knowing or feeling my true self.
Other crystals: Apophyllite & Peridot
Practice: Cast out

Pink Tourmaline

Citrine & Pink Tourmaline
FOR LIFE ACHE

Life can just feel hard and heavy sometimes. I believe we can get life ache – sometimes it's explainable, often not. Perhaps we've digested something dense that is struggling to dissolve and leave our system. Perhaps there is pain in the world our being feels is too hard to bear witness to or too difficult to comprehend. At times like these we need to learn to love again, to send love to ourselves and the world over. Pink Tourmaline allows us to dispel heavier matter seen or unseen within our being and with grace and ease, it moves us back to our feelings of love. The power couple becomes complete with Citrine, as she allows us to heighten the flow of the healing, moving all that is redundant back into the ether for clearing and by return magnetises the uplifted state we deserve to feel in an abundant fashion. A duo for when you feel like giving up and but the heart is kicking you to go on.

Mantra: When the storms come and the emotions flow, I have the strength to root deep and allow my heart to glow.
Other crystals: Rainbow Fluorite & Rose Quartz, Lemon Chrysoprase & Chrysocolla, Tiger's Eye & Pyrite
Practice: Clear the way

FOR TURNING THE 'I CAN'T' INTO 'HOW CAN I?'

The next section is for when we're feeling impatient. Impatience is usually based around the need to 'get there' or 'have it now', but the stress of forcing this energy can quickly turn into 'This is impossible' or 'I can't', just before you down tools and quit. When you start to feel this way, just know that it will always come and it will always go. In fact, it's an important part of the process because it can reveal to us the truth of the direction of flow of our energy. So, next time you're feeling a bit stuck, use these crystal transformers, to turn an impossible into a doable... Let's go do!

Lemon Chrysoprase
FOR GETTING CURIOUS

We can often feel alone or lonely on this path of manifestation and its practices, and that can be demotivating. We need to bring in vibrational energy that resonates with the unseen in the ether and taps into the go-getter within. When we feel driven, we feel inspired to the inner get up and go that's calling us, without being managed there by another human. Lemon Chrysoprase is a motivator, a driving force in times of 'going it alone'. It releases old cycles, filters your system and your habits and loudly assists in turning our minds to curiosity and exploration, and away from the old ways of doubt.

Mantra: I am ferociously curious about all that sets my world on fire.

Other crystals: Howlite, Scolecite, Carnelian, Garnet, Blue Aragonite

Lemon Chrysoprase

Rainbow Moonstone
FOR BELIEF WHEN WE FEEL TIME IS RUNNING OUT

Oh yes, that old chestnut – the time-ticking monkey. Let Rainbow Moonstone shine upon you, soothing the disappointment, bringing the magic back to that space where the time 'looks' like it's getting away from you and you start to think you have bet on the wrong horse. This sense limits our creative current and we have to let it move out our system. We cannot dwell on it because it's when we need the light the most, when we need to put the magic back into the work and rediscover our faith, even if it seems to be taking longer than we had imagined. Let Rainbow Moonstone remind you never to quit, let her guide you to be brave, to cleanse that lens of focus, to shine light on that which needs to be healed so you can feel brave enough to pick up again where you left off.

Mantra: Under your gaze I reignite the belief in mine.
Other crystals: Fire Agate, Pyrite, Quartz
Practice: Clear the way, Cast out

Fire Agate
FOR CLEANSING THE LENS

We often require different elements to cleanse our way and our being. Fire Agate is an important member of your tribe as he will regularly cleanse your vessel with his powerful vibrational heat, whilst keeping that smile on your face. He makes the shifts empowering, grounding and enlightening. With him in your grasp, answers tend to fall from thin air and you seemingly move at sonic speed but without discombobulation as you investigate scenarios and options for your growth. With these moving this fast, be sure to take time to plant those new seeds.

Mantra: I clear, I see, I move, I grow.
Other crystals: Iolite, Caribbean Calcite, Apophyllite, Labradorite
Practice: Clear the way

Selenite & Stromatolite
FOR HEIGHTENED CONNECTIVITY

When we are in true alignment, we tend to just 'know' things. Our spider senses are on high alert and often we can become a little complacent or cocky about our newfound abilities. They can become hard to maintain

Selenite

because we, somewhat egotistically, think they're coming from just us! In order to move within this heavenly flow of manifestation without fearing its loss, we have to acknowledge and connect with where it comes from – Mother Earth and the spirit in the sky, however that is known or felt to you. We are the teammate in between the two and the relationships within a team have to be tended to, right? Selenite allows us to shower our calls out into the universe, without limitation. It allows us to nurture and connect with angelic frequencies – we can go higher than our mind ever allows us to imagine in her forcefield and ethereal flow. Sometimes (more often than not) we feel the power of the casting out, but the calling in can feel muted which leads to impatience and a lack of commitment and focus. In order to manifest heaven to earth we have to ground the energies, but first ground ourselves in the feeling of that wave of manifestation coming. Stromatolite allows us to let that power and its answers engulf us without our ego inflating, allowing our power to be harnessed, rather than it harnessing us.

Mantra: Patience at feet, grace in my heart, eyes set to heaven, trusting in the time we are to start.
Other crystals: Scolecite & Tiger's Eye

PART 5

CLEANSING & RESETTING THE SCORE

Lapis Lazuli

Coming up are a few different ways you can cleanse and charge your crystals. However, before we get on to the how, we need to remember the why. There are a few reasons and I like to think of them as the three Rs:

- reset
- recharge
- reimagine

RESET

Crystals are amazing sponges for energy. When you bring your beautiful crystal home from the store for the first time, you must imagine that a million and one energies have touched your new pal before landing at your door – even just being in a box in transit, it's been soaking up energies on the go. So we always cleanse and charge our crystals when they are new to us, even if your friend has gifted it to you with much love – cleansing won't release the positive intention, only that which doesn't serve you and it. Equally, if you wish to pass on one of your crystals because the time feels right for it to move on, we cleanse with the intention of resetting it back to factory settings (much like your phone).

Mantra: Crystal clear as you can be, align now only to the energy of me.

RECHARGE

Just like us the crystals need a rest day – so even if you are in the throes of a manifestation practice or have attuned your pieces to a particular vibe or goal, we need to keep nurturing them whilst they're doing all the good work. Crystals will always work, even if we don't take the time to charge them, however they won't be buzzing at their highest potential.

You may already have a ritualistic practice for cleaning and charging – perhaps you do it monthly (or when you remember to!) with a full or new moon. You can add your working crystals to your regular cleanses or, if you sense they are feeling a little on the 'dull' side, put them in the sun and charge them with some of Mother Nature's fuel.

Mantra: Crystal power, with this cleanse you ignite the power to burn brighter than bright.

Selenite

REIMAGINE

Now perhaps you are working towards something powerful or BIG with your crystals and you want to add to the intention, or perhaps you have decided you have changed your mind all together. Don't worry, you can reimagine the intention of your crystal, repurpose and realign it without undoing or feeling you have lost time with all the work you have done so far.

Mantra: Crystal wise, crystal clear – cleanse the mirror of life that I hold near.

Below are my favourite ways to cleanse and charge – use the rest, recharge or reimagine mantra which feels most relevant to you when cleansing. Repeat the mantra three times as you start the cleansing process and again as you take the crystal (or crystals) to hand once the process is concluded.

WATER BATHING

Water is refreshing and reinvigorating for us and the crystals feel the same way. Nothing beats a good soak in water if they have been working hard for you or a quick shower if they just need a burst of life. So you may like to turn on the cool tap and rinse the crystals in your hands or you might prefer to place them in a sink or bowl of water and allow them to soak as you would yourself in a bath or in the sea.

You do not need any soaps or detergents. You can, however, add a teaspoon of Himalayan salts to a soak for that extra cleanse. Allow your crystals to dry on a natural fabric in daylight or by the light of the moon. I would use moonlight for those crystals that are more housebound and starting to gather a little dust internally as well as externally.

It is important to note that some crystals, such as Selenite, should not be placed in water as they will start to dissolve. Others cannot be soaked in water for prolonged periods of time, such as Malachite or Pyrite, as they will start to lose their shine.

SUN SHOWERS

The sun, that great ball of energy that touches us daily, the fire light that fuels the world and our very existence, moves through and warms even the hardest of materials. Just as we feel reenergised when we turn our faces up to the warm sun, so too do our crystals. I would suggest, for extra effect, showering or bathing your crystals and then moving them outside, not only to cleanse them, but to allow them to be fuelled by the sun's gentle rays. If you do not have access to outdoor space, the rays of the sun penetrating through a window are equally powerful. Observe how the crystals twinkle after being kissed by the sun and feel as its magic transmutes through them into your being.

Amazonite

MOON BATHS

The moon is shining upon us always, even when we can't see her. There is such comfort to be had in knowing you have a super champion shining upon you, governing the push and pull of all bodies of waters upon our fine planet. All emotion as energy is kindred to the element of water, so the moon, whether she is in a state of newness, fullness or waning, is pulling the currents, the tides, rivers and oceans, in us, and in our crystals. She draws out, pulls to the surface from our crystals all that they have been shifting from us. It's pure magic how Mama Moon removes the toxins from your charms and at the same time from yourself. It also offers you a regular cleansing cycle as she graces us in totality every lunar month without fail. Even when you can't see her behind the clouds, you can feel her presence. She has an incredibly special connection with crystals, as she does with all nature. Shower or soak your crystals in water and then lay them outside or on the windowsill to allow the moon to bathe them in her healing light.

CANDLE CHARGE

As always when working with fire, you need to take care. This is my quick-fix charge – think of it like plugging in your phone to top up the battery. If I've had a toxic day or I've been exposed to some unwanted or unexpected bad vibes, I will always cross my crystal through the very tip of a candle flame. You don't need to hold it too close for the heat to burn off the bad energy. Pass it through once or twice and then place it on a natural surface such as cloth, sand, soil or Himalayan salts, to ground it and to allow it to settle and soak in the recharge.

SMOKE IT OUT

Palo Santo and smudge sticks such as sage are fantastic – the smoke from these beauties goes to the negative or heavier energy and lifts it up and out of your way. Light the smudge stick as instructed on the packaging and allow the smoke to pass gently over your crystal collection. I like to do this in a circular motion (for completion) or two figures of eight (for universal infinite connection). The smoke from the smudge stick will track down the negativity, much like a trained sniffer dog, and chase it out of town.

Bumble Bee Jasper

Pyrite

THE CONCLUSION (THAT IS NOT A CONCLUSION)

I can't really conclude this book because there is no end point to what you are creating through manifesting. Manifesting is not something to be learned, it's something you were born doing, you simply need to realign the vibe.

As such, you will read this book with one manifestation intention in mind and then reopen it days, weeks, maybe years later, and cast out a new spell. As your energy uplifts, as your vision of and belief in life and self evolves, you'll come back to it with a different lens. What a divine blessing it is to be so much more in control of our own life or to take back control of it, so please enjoy it – what fun and what power, right?

We need to remember that feeling is believing; that our energy, thoughts, outlook, inner orbit, connections, relationships, 'things', and so on, are able to be changed and it's well within our power to do that if we can practise the magnetic art and energetic alignment of manifesting.

Please always keep in mind that the results of the effort in your practice – the commitment you make or have made to yourself by reading this book and working with your crystals – have already, in an instant, shifted you into another gear of creation. In doing this for yourself you have already enabled (or manifested) the creation of a brighter, richer tapestry of life experience and reward.

Some days will be brighter than others, that's the experience of life. We can't obliterate the days when the rain falls, nor should we curse them – we need merely change the lens of focus (there are crystals everywhere for that!). We can then feel and see the blessing in what the rain brings us; what

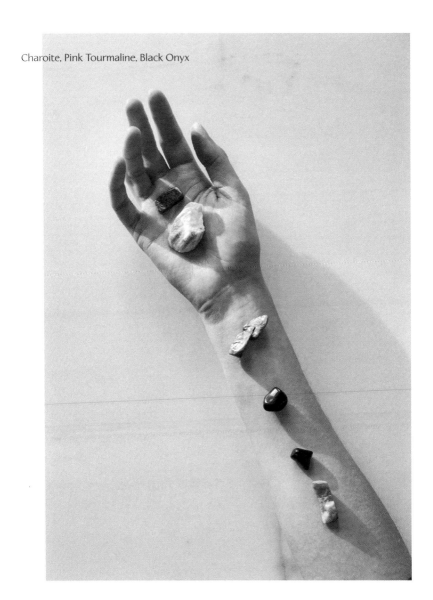

Charoite, Pink Tourmaline, Black Onyx

it's washing away and how it is assisting us to grow. Move the attention and clear the energy, then jump back into the power of manifesting flow.

We need to remember that the manifestation movement is not just a speedy fix, helping us catch a quick win or a fleeting high. We must always work on what we are truly endeavouring to bring into being and to tune into whether it's for our upmost good – the ultimate potential of the purest kind; only then will it be. If something feels stuck, use your crystals to guide you as you ask, 'Where am I in my own way?', 'What can I shift?' or 'What do I need to tweak in the process?' and 'Is what I am manifesting in alignment with who I am or who I am becoming?'.

Remember this work – this art – doesn't all come from the power of the mind, you don't simply 'think' things into being. That belief is what would make this practice just another flash-in-the-pan trend. You are a multi-layered, wonderous amalgamation of energy, experience, thoughts and feelings – past, present and future. Some of those vibrations, beliefs and mindsets, and the energy they create, work to keep you safe by inadvertently throwing you out and off your flow. So when you feel frustrated or you don't know why you just aren't getting it, or that manifesting doesn't work for you because you are not good enough, move that energy into reaching out to the universe, and reaching for your crystals the right one will always grab you. They are your lenses: they purify, align your being and your energy with what inherently feels good, helping you to manifest more of that feel-good and bring it into your physical life. Your crystals are supersonic universal keys that allow you not only to access the abundance of flow in the universe, they also unlock all that no longer serves you. They flush out the thoughts and associated energetic effects of low-lying energies weighing you down, clearing the way to enlighten you. They give you crystal clear focus.

You are the master of your own destiny. You are powerful and you deserve what you are dreaming of. As we explore the art of crystal manifesting, crystal aligning and high vibing we come to recognise that this creates the soundtrack of your life. Practise the rhythm, stay dedicated to the focus of your own tune, your own lane of manifestation and intention and tend to it every day. Ask yourself how clear the path is. How good do the harmonies of what you are calling in sound and feel like together? How honest are you being with why you want it? How clear are you being with what you have outgrown? Be consistent with the feeling of what you are seeking to manifest and let it bloom from within you.

You have always and you are aways manifesting you. You've done an epic job so far, this is merely the next level you've been manifesting for...

Tourmalated Quartz, Citrine, Golden Healer, Rainbow Fluorite, Tiger's Eye,
Hematite, Flower Agate, Apatite

Apatite, Apophyllite

RESOURCES, PRACTITIONERS & STOCKISTS

If you would like to work with me and my crystal squad further to learn more about yours or yourself from them, then drop me a line, say hello and find out the multitude of ways we can work together. It would be a blessing to see you in person.

You can find me and my bespoke collection of hand-charged and intention-set crystals, Emma Lucy Rocks, at **www.emmalucyknowles.com**

As with your crystals, different energies require different vibrations and as such, I felt it important to share some of the fab beings who have worked their magic on my energy over the years, be that through energy, crystal or sound work or through the crystals they source. If you are reading this and feel the draw to any of these angels – I could not be happier for you, honestly, they are all epic – lean into the pull, trust your intuition and enjoy their magic on your energetical manifestation journey.

PRACTITIONERS

Energy Healers, Crystal Sound Therapists, Acupuncturists

Jane
Guardian of the Soul, Healer & Acupuncturist
janecarlton10@gmail.com

Rita Hiri
Energy & Number Healing
www.systemofnumbers.com

Jasmine Hamsbro at Emerald and Tiger
Reiki, Sound Healing
www.emeraldandtiger.com

Selda Goodwin
Psychic Healing & Certified Healing Training
seldasoulspace.com
@seldasoulspace

Debs Duke
Crystal Healing, Reiki
nerinatreatments@gmail.com

Mayra at Sound Alchemy
Sound Healing, Quantum Healing, Breath Work
mayra@mayrasoulalchemy.com
@mayra.soul.alchemy

——

Sam Powey-Hall at IO Project
Sound Meditation in Unique Locations
@IOProjectHQ

——

Cal Wansbrough at Yoga in the Big Smoke
Acupuncture & Yin Yoga
www.yogainthebigsmoke.co.uk

——

Ross Barr at Ross J Barr
Acupuncture
www.rossbarr.com

——

Kathy Fortescue
Clinical Hypnotherapy
www.kathyfortescuehypnotherapy.com

ONLINE COMMUNITIES & APPS

www.gaia.com
www.wyldemoon.co.uk
www.wimhofmethod.com
www.therisingcircle.com

CRYSTALS, CLEANSING TOOLS
& OTHER RESOURCES

Online:

Emma Lucy Rocks www.emmalucyknowles.com

The Colourful Dot www.thecolourfuldot.com

Moon Mist & Crystals www.paoloreflex.com

Tinkalink www.tinkalink.com

Lit By Lucy www.litbylucy.com

Ume www.ume-collection.co.uk

Get Lit Retreat www.getlitretreat.com

Downdog & Crow www.downdogcrow.co.uk

In-store and online:

The Astrology Store www.londonastrology.com

Bamford www.bamford.com

Mysteries www.mysteries.co.uk

Dale Rogers Ammonite www.dalerogersammonite.com

—

Mama Moon www.mamamooncandles.com

—

Soulstice London www.soulsticelondon.com

—

Venusrox www.venusrox.com

Online stockists to Europe, North America, Australia and New Zealand:

Emma Lucy Knowles www.emmalucyknowles.com

—

The Colourful Dot http://thecolourfuldot.com

—

Wilde Ones http://www.wildeones.com

—

Shamans Crystal http://www.shamanscrystal.co.uk

—

Holistic Shop http://www.holisticshop.co.uk

Image opposite: Tiger's eye, Apatite, Tourmalated Quartz, Hematite, Fluorite, Flower Agate, Golden Healers, Citrine

FURTHER READING

Reading is an enlightening tool – it lifts our mood, our consciousness, just by directing or showing the mind the path through. These are the books that have helped me on my life, crystal and manifestation journey. May they serve you as well.

MANIFESTATION

- *The Game of Life and How to Play It*, Florence Scovel-Shinn

- *Ask and It Is Given*, Esther and Jerry Hicks

- *A Course in Miracles*, Foundation for Inner Peace

CRYSTALS

- *The Power of Crystal Healing*, Emma Lucy Knowles

- *The Crystal Bible*, Judy Hall

- *Crystal Grids Handbook*, Judy Hall

- *The Inner Beauty Bible*, Laurey Simmons

SOUL WORK

- *Many Lives, Many Masters*, Dr Brian Weiss

- *Polishing The Mirror,* Ram Dass

- *The Celestine Prophecy*, James Redfield

- *You Can Heal Your Life*, Louise L. Hay

- *You Are a Rainbow*, Emma Lucy Knowles

- *The Life Changing Power of Intuition*, Emma Lucy Knowles

- *Fear*, Osho

- *Be Here Now*, Ram Dass

Rose Quartz

Crazy Lace Agate

INDEX

By crystal

Amazonite, Stromatolite, Sunstone, Charoite

INDEX

By manifestation intention

Amethyst Geode

qi 17

realigning the path 115
receiving, the art of 86
recharging crystals 141, 143
reflections, positive 79
reimagining crystals 141,
    144–5
resetting crystals 141, 142
romance, manifesting 92

sacral chakra 62
sage 150
the self
  the art of receiving 86
  for becoming 79–80
  breakthrough energy
    flow 84
  expanding our knowledge
    of 79
  good vibrations 77
  higher self 80
  manifesting the self 75–89
  manifesting your glow 83
  for personal space 86–7
  positive reflections 79
  reflecting your true self 79
  self love 75–6

transforming worry into
  worth 76
trust and confidence 80–1
unconditional love and
  self worth 91
shining your light 116
sleep 67
  calling in practice while
    asleep 67
smoking crystals 150
smudge sticks 150
social comfort 123–4
solar plexus chakra 61
space, personal 86–7
The Spirit 137
standing out 116
sunlight
  breakthrough energy
    flow 84
  cleansing crystals with
    145, 146
  manifesting 77

third eye chakra 59
thoughts
  energy and 12
  flow of 58
throat chakra 59

Hematite

Image overleaf: Spirit Quartz, Malachite, Apophyllite, Blue Calcite,
Fire Quartz, Lapis Lazuli

ABOUT THE AUTHOR

Emma Lucy Knowles is a clairvoyant and intuitive hands-on spiritual and energy healer, crystal reader, meditation teacher and author. Emma Lucy started her exploration of her spiritual 'skills' at the tender age of 7 years old having suffered with a bout of childhood depression as a result of her heightened sensitivities and powerful unexplained senses – she had a difficulty in learning how to become, understand and communicate herself in a world in which she was striving far too hard to be 'normal'.

Subsequently living what she describes as a very 'full life' made of enriching experiences – Emma Lucy has set about transforming her life pains into power, and in turn making this life's work a power to benefit all. She helps people and souls worldwide to discover and uncover their own power, how to overcome and transmute their pains, in their own way and in their own time, into heart felt success. Using her own life and experience, the power of energy and the power of crystals, she helps to guide and gather a powerful crowd of what she lovingly calls The Overcomers.

Website: www.emmalucyknowles.com
Instagram: @your_emmalucy

Apophyllite, Fire Quartz, Selenite

THANK YOUS

I wanted to start by saying thank you to you for reading this book, for embracing her and the crystals into your manifested life – that means more to me than you'll ever know.

To my family like no other, Jen the Hen, AK, Bec and Dolly, for your endless everything, the most generous beings I could ever have been blessed to be familied with – thank you! To the beloved, the guardians, to Gaia, to my squad in spirit: Chris, Tom, Lily, Eric, Dani, Lady P, Trev, Mary, George and beyond – what life would be without you I do not know, thank you for showing me just how endless love truly is.

To the book legends. Celia, you are the publisher of dreams. To the creative genies Imogen, Tamsin, Louise, Lizzie, Sophie and Louie – thank you so much for all your talents – what brilliance you bring independently and collaboratively!

To the legend that is Barry and the team at the Astrology Store in London's Covent Garden. For your crystals, your generosity and general brilliance in bringing this book to life. Thank you!

To all the beautiful, brilliant friends and beautiful, brilliant souls I get to work and walk this life with – thank you for all the blessings and to those who brought the harder lessons, I thank you. Without learning, there is no knowing, without knowing, there is no wisdom and without wisdom there is nothing.

Please remember that crystals are complementary to, and not a replacement for, any medical treatment you may be receiving. If in doubt, speak to your medical adviser.

1

Ebury Press, an imprint of Ebury Publishing
20 Vauxhall Bridge Road
London SW1V 2SA

Ebury Press is part of the Penguin Random House group of companies whose addresses can be found at global.penguinrandomhouse.com

Penguin
Random House
UK

First published by Ebury Press in 2023

www.penguin.co.uk

A CIP catalogue record for this book is available from the British Library

ISBN 9781529905373

Design: Louise Evans
Photographer: Lizzie Mayson
Props: Louie Waller
With thanks to the Astrology Shop for lending their amazing collection of crystals.

Colour reproduction by AltaImage London
Printed and bound in Lativa by Livonia Print SIA

The authorised representative in the EEA is Penguin Random House Ireland, Morrison Chambers, 32 Nassau Street, Dublin D02 YH68.

Penguin Random House is committed to a sustainable future for our business, our readers and our planet. This book is made from Forest Stewardship Council® certified paper.

MIX
Paper | Supporting
responsible forestry
FSC® C018179